DATE DUE

PowerKids Readers:

The Bilingual Library of the United States of America

TEXAS

JOSÉ MARÍA OBREGÓN

Traducción al español: Mauricio Velázquez de León

The Rosen Publishing Group's
PowerKids Press™ & **Editorial Buenas Letras**™
New York

Published in 2005 by The Rosen Publishing Group, Inc.
29 East 21st Street, New York, NY 10010

First Edition

Photo Credits: Cover © Vince Streano/Corbis; p. 5 © Joseph Sohm/The Image Works; p. 9 © David Muench/Getty Images; p. 11 © David Muench/Corbis; pp. 13, 31 (Katherine Anne Porter, Lyndon B. Johnson, Joan Crawford) © Bettmann/Corbis; p. 15 Courtesy of Mission Espiritu Santo, Goliad State Park, Texas Parks and Wildlife Department, photo by Dallas Hoppestad; p. 17 © Brooks Kraft/Corbis; p. 19 © Bob Daemmrich/Corbis; p. 21 © David Stoecklein/Corbis; p. 23 © Richard Cummins/Corbis; p. 25 © Larry Lee Photography/Corbis; p. 31 (Dwight Eisenhower) © Corbis, p. 31 (Sandra Day O'Connor) © Wally McNamee/Corbis, p. 31 (Selena) © Mitchell Gerber/Corbis, p. 31 (Astronaut) © NASA/JSC, p. 31 (Cowboy) © Richard Hamilton Smith/Corbis, p. 31 (Farmland) © Terry W. Eggers/Corbis

Library of Congress Cataloging-in-Publication Data

Obregón, José María, 1963-
Texas / José María Obregón ; traducción al español, Mauricio Velázquez de Leon.– 1st ed.
    p. cm. – (The bilingual library of the United States of America)
Includes index.
ISBN 1-4042-3109-9 (library binding)
1. Texas–Juvenile literature. I. Title. II. Series.
F386.3.O27 2005
976.4–dc22
                                                     2004027125

Manufactured in the United States of America

Due to the changing nature of Internet links, Editorial Buenas Letras has developed an online list of Web sites related to the subject of this book. This site is updated regularly. Please use this link to access the list:

http://www.buenasletraslinks.com/ls/texas

Contents

Contenido

Welcome to Texas

Texas is the second–largest state in the United States. Texas is known as the Lone Star State.

Bienvenidos a Texas

Por su tamaño, Texas es el segundo estado de los Estados Unidos. A Texas se le llama el Estado de la Estrella Solitaria.

The Texas Flag and the State Seal

La bandera y el escudo de Texas

Texas Geography

Texas is one of the southwestern states, along with Arizona, New Mexico, and Oklahoma.

Geografía de Texas

Texas es uno de los estados del suroeste. Arizona, Nuevo México y Oklahoma también están en el suroeste.

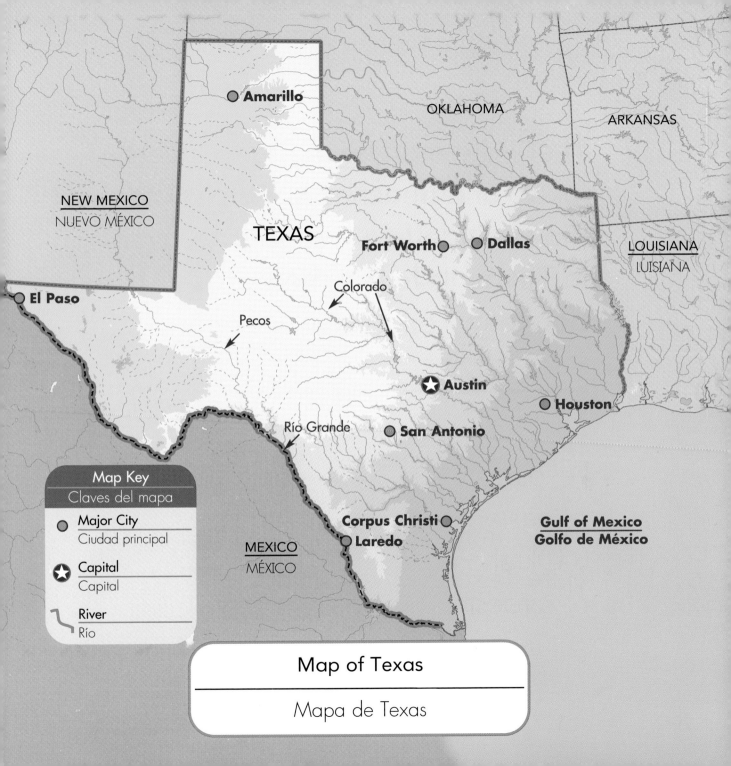

NEW MEXICO
NUEVO MÉXICO

OKLAHOMA

ARKANSAS

LOUISIANA
LUISIANA

● Amarillo

TEXAS

Fort Worth ●   ● Dallas

Colorado

El Paso

Pecos

★ Austin

● Houston

Río Grande

● San Antonio

MEXICO
MÉXICO

Corpus Christi ●

● Laredo

Gulf of Mexico
Golfo de México

Map Key
Claves del mapa

● **Major City**
Ciudad principal

★ **Capital**
Capital

River
Río

Map of Texas

Mapa de Texas

There are many mountains, rivers, lakes, and beaches in Texas. The Río Grande is a well-known river in Texas. It forms the border between Texas and Mexico.

Texas tiene muchas montañas, ríos, lagos y playas. El Río Grande es un río muy conocido. Es la frontera entre Texas y México.

A View of the Río Grande

___

Una vista del Río Grande

Texas History

Texas was part of Mexico for many years. Texas and Mexico went to war in 1836. A well-known battle was fought here at the Alamo mission.

Historia de Texas

Durante varios años Texas formó parte de México. En 1836 Texas y México se declararon en guerra. Una famosa batalla se llevó a cabo aquí, en la misión de El Álamo.

The Alamo Mission in San Antonio, Texas

La misión de El Álamo en San Antonio Texas

Davy Crockett was a hero of the Alamo. Davy Crockett died fighting for Texas. He lived from 1786 to 1836.

Davy Crockett fue uno de los héroes de El Álamo. Davy Crockett murió defendiendo a Texas. Crockett vivió desde 1786 hasta 1836.

Davy Crockett

Francisca Álvarez is known as the Angel of Goliad. She saved the lives of 20 American soldiers during the Battle of Goliad. This battle happened in 1836, during the Texas Revolution.

Francisca Álvarez es conocida como el Ángel de Goliad. Francisca salvó la vida de 20 estadounidenses durante la batalla de Goliad. Esta batalla sucedió en 1836, durante la Revolución Texana.

Francisca Álvarez

George W. Bush grew up in Midland and Houston, Texas. He became governor of Texas in 1994. He served as president of the United States twice, in 2000 and 2004.

George W. Bush creció en Midland y en Houston, Texas. Fue gobernador de Texas en 1994, y presidente de los Estados Unidos en dos ocasiones, en 2000 y 2004.

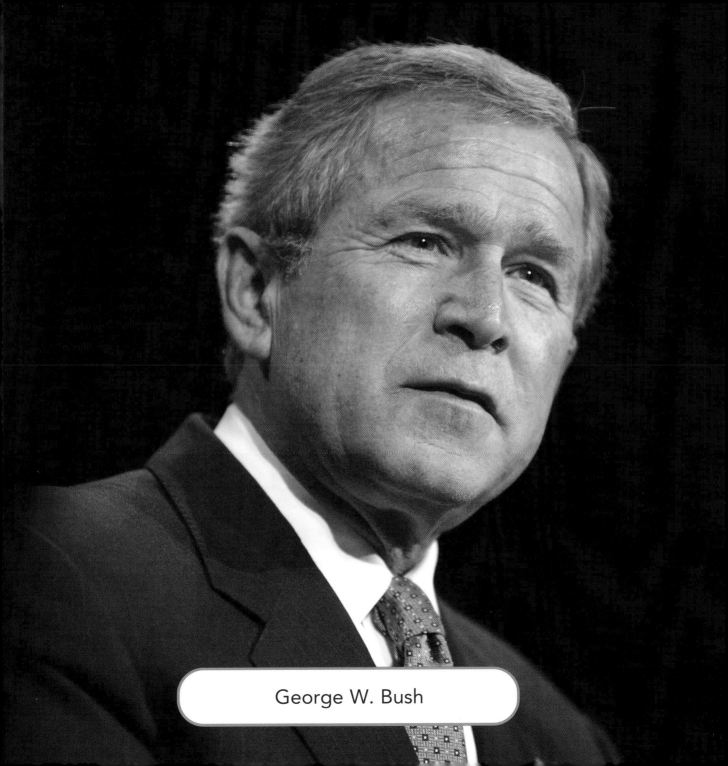

George W. Bush

Living in Texas

People from many different countries have made Texas their home. Texans love to have parties. Dancing is part of many holidays.

La vida en Texas

Personas de muchos países distintos viven en Texas. A los texanos les encantan sus fiestas. Muchas fiestas se celebran con danzas.

Mexican Dance in San Antonio

Danza mexicana en San Antonio

Cowboys are well-known in Texas. Cowboys wear hats and work on ranches. Many children want to be cowboys when they grow up.

Los vaqueros son muy conocidos en Texas. Los vaqueros usan sombreros y trabajan en los ranchos. Muchos niños quieren ser vaqueros cuando sean grandes.

A Cowboy Family in Texas

Una familia de vaqueros en Texas

Texas Today

The Johnson Space Center is in Houston, Texas. The space center is a fun place to visit. Here you can see how astronauts live and work in space.

Texas hoy

El Centro Espacial Johnson está en la ciudad de Houston, Texas. El centro espacial es un lugar muy divertido. Aquí puedes ver cómo viven y trabajan los astronautas en el espacio.

Visitors to the Johnson Space Center

Visitantes en el Centro Espacial Johnson

Houston, Dallas, San Antonio, El Paso, and Austin are important cities in Texas. Austin is the capital of the state of Texas.

Houston, Dallas, San Antonio, El Paso y Austin son ciudades importantes de Texas. Austin es la capital del estado de Texas.

The Capitol Building in Austin

Edificio del capitolio en la ciudad de Austin

Activity:
Let´s Draw the Texas Flag

Actividad:
Dibujemos la bandera de Texas

Begin your flag with a rectangle.

Comienza tu bandera con un rectángulo.

Next draw a vertical line on the left side of the flag.

Ahora dibuja una línea vertical en el lado izquierdo de tu bandera.

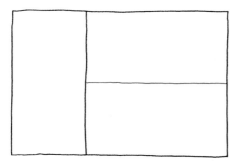

Add a horizontal line across the middle of the right side of the flag.

Añade una línea horizontal en el lado derecho de la bandera.

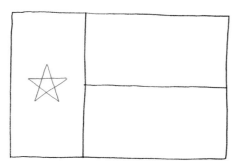

Draw a five-pointed star in the left side of your flag.

Dibuja una estrella de cinco puntas en el lado izquierdo de tu bandera.

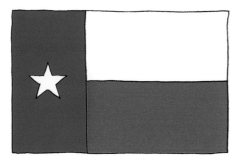

Color in your flag.

Colorea tu bandera.

Timeline | Cronología

	Timeline	Cronología
1519	Alonso Álvarez de Pineda sails into the Rio Grande and maps the coast of Texas.	Alonso Álvarez de Pineda navega el Río Grande y traza el mapa de la costa de Texas.
1821	Texas becomes a state within the Republic of Mexico.	Texas pasa a ser un estado de la República Mexicana.
1836	Texas soldiers defend the Alamo. Texas wins its independence.	Los soldados texanos defienden el Álamo. Texas gana su independencia.
1845	Texas becomes the twenty-eighth state of the Union.	Texas se convierte en el vigésimo octavo estado de la Unión.
1861	The Civil War begins. Texas separates from the Union.	Comienza la Guerra Civil. Texas se separa de la Unión.
1870	Texas is admitted back into the Union.	El estado de Texas es admitido nuevamente en la Unión.
1964	The Johnson Space Center opens in Houston	El Centro Espacial Johnson se inaugura en Houston.

Texas Events

January
Texas Citrus Festival in Mission

February
Charro Days Festival in Brownsville

March
Texas Independence Day, 2

April
Fiesta San Antonio en San Antonio
San Jacinto Day, 21

May
Cinco de Mayo Celebration, 5

July
Shakespeare Festival in Odessa
Texas Cowboy Reunion and
Rodeo in Stamford

September
Mexican Independence Day, 16
State Fair in Dallas

October
Texas Rose Festival in Tyler

December
Festival of the Lights in San Antonio

Eventos en Texas

Enero
Festival de los cítricos en Misión

Febrero
Festival del día del charro en Brownsville

Marzo
Día de la Independencia de Texas, 2

Abril
Fiesta de San Antonio en San Antonio
Día de San Jacinto, 21

Mayo
Celebración del Cinco de Mayo, 5

Julio
Festival Shakespeare en Odessa
Reunión de vaqueros y rodeo de Texas
en Stamford

Septiembre
Día de la Independencia de México, 16
Feria del estado en Dallas

Octubre
Festival de la rosa de Texas en Tyler

Diciembre
Festival de las luces en San Antonio

Texas Facts/Datos sobre Texas

Population
21 million

Población
21 millones

Capital
Austin

Capital
Austin

State motto
Friendship

Lema del estado
Amistad

State Flower
Bluebonnet

Flor del estado
Lupino

State Bird
Mockingbird

Ave del estado
Zensontle

State Nickname
The Lone Star State

Mote del estado
El Estado de la Estrella Solitaria

State Tree
Pecan

Árbol del estado
Nogal

State Song
"Texas Our Texas"

Canción del estado
"Texas, nuestro Texas"

State Gemstone
Blue Topaz

Piedra preciosa
Topacio azul

Famous Texans/Texanos famosos

Dwight Eisenhower
(1890–1969)

U.S. president

Presidente de los E.U.A.

Katherine Anne Porter
(1890–1980)

Author

Escritora

Lyndon B. Johnson
(1908–1973)

U.S. president

Presidente de los E.U.A

Joan Crawford
(1908–1977)

Actress

Actriz

Sandra Day O'Connor
(1930–)

Supreme Court justice

Juez de la Suprema Corte

Selena
(1971–1995)

Singer

Cantante

Words to Know/Palabras que debes saber

astronaut
astronauta

border
frontera

cowboy
vaquero

farmland
tierras de cultivo

Here are more books to read about Texas:
Otros libros que puedes leer sobre Texas:

In English/En inglés:
Texas
By Alexandra Hanson-Harding
Children's Press, 2001

In Spanish/En español:
Texas, el estado de la estrella solitaria
por: Barenblat, Rachael.
Traducción: Victory Productions
World Almanac Library, 2004

Words in English: 247   Palabras en español: 273

Index

Índice